PATRIOTIC ECONOMICS:

HOW TO THRIVE WHILE HELPING AMERICA

JEFFREY A. ROSENSWEIG

With Lori Sullivan

FOREWORD BY KEN BLANCHARD

PATRIOTIC ECONOMICS:
HOW TO THRIVE WHILE HELPING AMERICA
COPYRIGHT © 2001 BY JEFFREY A. ROSENSWEIG

ISBN: 0-937539-60-0

EXECUTIVE BOOKS
206 WEST ALLEN STREET
MECHANICSBURG, PA 17055
1-800-233-2665
WWW.EXECUTIVEBOOKS.COM

PRINTED IN THE UNITED STATES OF AMERICA

Executive
Books

Let us have faith that right makes might, and in that faith, let us, to the end, dare to do our duty as we understand it.
Abraham Lincoln, 1860

You must be the change you wish to see in the world.
Mahatma Gandhi

TABLE OF CONTENTS

☆ ☆ ☆ ☆ ☆

Far better it is to dare mighty things, to win glorious triumphs, even though checkered by failure, than to take rank with those poor spirits who neither enjoy much nor suffer much, because they live in the gray twilight that knows not victory nor defeat.

President Theodore Roosevelt, 1899

Foreword

by Ken Blanchard

Harness your fear...Fear kills more people than death.
General George S. Patton

The mind is an incredible instrument. In fact, it's too bad that we didn't get an owner's manual when we got ours. A lot of people don't realize that the mind and computer are a lot alike. Neither the mind nor the computer knows the difference between the truth and what you tell it. If you put information in the computer, it doesn't ask you where you got those figures nor does it tell you if those figures are wrong. Instead, the computer does whatever it can with the information you give it. For years on end with the computer, we have said "garbage in and garbage out."

The same is true of the mind. The mind does not know the difference between the truth and what you tell it. If you get up in the morning and look in the mirror and say, "You are fabulous!" your mind doesn't say "Who are you kidding, I know you better than that!" No, your mind believes you. If you fill your mind with positive thoughts, it will not reject them or replace them with negative thoughts.

As an aftermath of September 11, we all have to ask ourselves, "How are we programming our minds, not only to survive but thrive in these crucial times?" How we answer that question will determine whether we are the next "greatest generation" or not. What made the "greatest generation?" They just thought differently. They never let fear enter their minds.

My father was a product of that generation. He graduated from the Naval Academy in 1924. With the ending of World War I, everybody felt that we had just fought and won the war to end all wars. So the nation felt it didn't need many military officers. As a result, my father was released from any military obligation at the end of the senior cruise. So, in January 1925, he entered Harvard Business School. Upon graduation in 1927, he began his career on Wall Street.

In 1940, when I was only one year old, he came home one day and announced to my mother, "I quit today." She said, "You did what?" He said, "I quit." At that time, he was being groomed as a vice president for a major New York City bank, so you can imagine her shock. He said to her, "Hitler is crazy and it is only a matter of time before the Japanese get into the war, so I rejoined the navy."

That day, my father went from a high-level management position to a Lieutenant in the navy. They stationed him at the Brooklyn Navy Yard. When the

Japanese bombed Pearl Harbor and brought the US into World War II, it looked like my father would spend the entire war, because of lack of field experience, in Brooklyn. He called an old friend of his who had stayed in the navy after they had graduated together from the Naval Academy. When my father called him he said, "What have you got for an old guy with no experience?" His friend called my dad back two days later and said, "Ted, all I have for someone with your background is a high-risk assignment. We need someone to command twelve LCI's (Landing Craft Infantry) that will be protecting the marines and the frogmen (known as the Seals today) when we attack the Marshall Islands."

The Marshall Islands attack was the "Normandy version" of Asia. My father took command of those twelve LCI's to defend the country he loved. At one point, there was a picture of my dad in *Time* magazine performing a funeral service for some of his men who were killed by missiles from our big ships that had fallen short of the target. That's how close to the beach my dad's ships were. It was so risky and so hazardous that seventy-five percent of his men were killed and/or wounded.

What caused people like my father and many others to step up to the challenge to become the greatest generation? It was Pearl Harbor. In many ways, September 11 is the new Pearl Harbor for us in the 21st century. How we respond to this tragedy will depend on how we think. If we fill our minds with fear about our safety and/or our economy, we could defeat ourselves.

That's why I think Jeff Rosensweig's book, *Patriotic Economics*, is so timely and important. As a nation we have to get into a positive mindset, and this book will show us how we can do that and help America and ourselves thrive in these trying times.

No longer can we sit around and wait for the President to act or Greenspan to act or our institutions to act – they all have to help and they are helping now. But every single individual has to look in the mirror and say, "What am I going to do to contribute?" This is no longer a world where we can depend on a patriarch or a few people making all the decisions for our own benefit. We need to take action ourselves. Like my father did so many years ago, it is time for each of us to step up and do what we can for our country. We must take action not only for the US economy and our personal finances, but also, to reach out to people in our own culture, of different cultures, of different religions, of different backgrounds – to show that love works better than hatred and compassion is better than violence.

I ask people all the time, "Would you like to make the world a better place for your having been here?" and everybody answers "Yes!" Then I say, "What's your plan?" and they all smile and look blank because they don't have a plan. Well, I want to tell you that *Patriotic Economics* is offering us a plan on how we can make the world a better place based on what we do and how we step up to the plate as individuals to protect our economy, to protect our freedom, and to show the world that we are not going to back off from what we believe in and what made this a great country. Thanks Jeff.

Ken Blanchard
Co-author, *The One Minute Manager*
and Co-author, *Mission Possible –*
Becoming a World-Class Organization
While There's Still Time

ACKNOWLEDGMENTS

First, I want to acknowledge those who inspired this book: the people who lost their lives in NY, DC, and Pennsylvania, and their grieving families along with the ordinary citizens who rose up to search and support. Your goodness and courage and faith will be an enduring legacy.

Second, I thank those who stood shoulder-to-shoulder with me as we rushed to produce and distribute this book, in the hope it can guide actions that can heal and can secure prosperity. There are good reasons why Ken Blanchard is arguably the top author and keynote speaker in business, and why Charlie Jones is called by all "Tremendous."

Likewise, good parts of this book owe much to my fellow Emory instructor, Lori Sullivan. Lori is an important researcher and writer on all my books, thus she is justifiably on the cover of this book. She graduated from Cornell University in 1991 and completed an MBA at Emory in 1998.

Pete Contrucci, Bettye Neal, Randi Strumlauf, Sandy Medina, David Wessels, Michelle Baker, Ashley Preisinger, Crystal Mario, Shezhad Mian, Eric Levin, and Simon Tripp also contributed selflessly. Mark Bell, a Marshall scholar now teaching at Oxford University, volunteered brilliant contributions.

Third, my colleagues at CNN Headlines News inspired many of the ideas here. President Teya Ryan provided me the opportunity to be a daily economic commentator for Headline News. Teya's wisdom became abundantly clear to me in those dark days in September 2001 when, as a commentator but not an employee of CNN, I had the freedom to speak out against fear, intolerance, and actions that could give satisfaction to terrorists by compounding their impact on the US economy and our enviable standard of living.

I want to express gratitude to my mentors at CNN. I thank Gail Evans for "discovering" me. Judy Milestone, Senior Vice President in charge of Research and Guest Booking for CNN, has been a constant friend and mentor at CNN. Executive Producers Charlie Moore, Alan Schrack, Jason Evans, and James Broyles helped me evolve my realistic, yet patriotic and positive, message. The same can be said for anchors Judy Fortin, Robin Meade, Charles Molineaux, Rudi Bakhtiar, Chuck Roberts, Linda Stouffer, and Kathleen Kennedy, among other stars.

Fourth, I thank Major General Perry Smith and Howard Gardner, two members of my ethical braintrust who provided key help on this book. Ken Breeden and Jackie Rohosky and their colleagues at the Georgia Department of Technical and Adult Education also contributed.

Fifth, I thank my mentors, exemplary leaders all, including Nobel Laureate James Tobin, Jan Leschly, Arthur Blank, Ambassador James Laney, Vicki Escarra, Bishop

Eddie Long, Tom Haggai, Joel Koblentz, John Robson, Tom Robertson, Rudi Dornbusch, Dan Amos, Hattie Hill, Tom Chapman, Mylle Mangum, Jim Blanchard, Charles Brady, Don Keough, Bernie Marcus, Jim Fowler and Dan Cathy.

Finally, terrorists unwittingly deepened our love of country, freedom, justice, and family. My wife, daughter, son and extended family remind me how fortunately blessed I have been, including having this opportunity to join Ken Blanchard and Charlie Jones in donating some proceeds from this book to charity.

INTRODUCTION

The world was indelibly altered on September 11, 2001. Freedom lovers and patriots worldwide came to the realization that we are engaged in the first war of the new millennium. It is not only a war against terrorism, but also a war against intolerance. It is a war for freedom and security, and a war against psychological and economic depression. Inspired by the heroic actions of so many firefighters, police, healthcare workers, and ordinary citizens who rose up as one united community, I have rushed to provide this book. All who have contributed here have one goal: to help patriotic individuals secure the prosperity and freedom of the US and our allies.

The war against terror and intolerance will be a long one. Indeed, the battle against terrorism and intolerance has been fought for centuries. Now, the escalation of the battle to a full-fledged war will involve, along with allied support, the full strength of the US military and intelligence agencies. This team, with a unified nation behind it, is the greatest force for freedom the world has ever witnessed. It will also entail crucial social, financial, and economic programs that will ultimately secure a lasting peace by fighting poverty and intolerance globally.

Fortunately, the US has a track record of winning wars and the subsequent struggles for peace and prosperity.

After World War II, the US embarked on the most noble act in history, the Marshall Plan, rebuilding both our allies and former enemies. Named after Secretary of State George Catlett Marshall, the original Marshall Plan inspires us to call for a new Marshall Plan – one FOR the US and its allies. The original Marshall Plan led to a *pax Americana* for the second half of the 20th century. We could certainly use some of the vision and moral courage of General Marshall as we fight the first war of the new century. And we may very well have it in Secretary of State Colin Powell, cited by many leaders, including my friend Major General Perry Smith, as embodying many of the noble traits of General Marshall.

In my favorite book on leadership, *Leading Minds* by Howard Gardner (Basic Books, 1995), the author enlightens us about Marshall in a chapter entitled, "George C. Marshall: The Embodiment of the Good Soldier." In it, Gardner portrays Marshall as an exemplary role model. First, Gardner states [p. 161], "In a commencement address of historic importance, delivered at Harvard University in June 1947, Marshall laid out the dimensions of such an effort. He declared:

It is logical that the United States should do whatever it is able to do to assist in the return of normal economic health in the world, without which there can be no political stability and no assured peace. Our policy is directed not against any country or doctrine but against hunger, poverty, desperation, and chaos. Its purpose should be the revival of a working economy in the world so as to permit the emergence of political and social conditions in which free institutions can exist."

Gardner succinctly summarizes why Marshall serves as a role model for much of today's military and civilian leadership [pp. 162-63].

In 1953, he received the Nobel Peace Prize. A singular experience for a person whose initial fame derived from his prosecution of the most destructive war in human history. The Nobel Committee spoke of the "most constructive peaceful work . . . in this century."

. . .

. . .Truman pronounced him "the greatest military man that this country ever produced – or any other country for that matter" and concluded, "The more I see and talk to him, the more certain I am he is the great one of the age." Secretary of War Henry Stimson declared, "I have seen a great many soldiers in my life, and you, sir, are the finest soldier I have ever known." *Time* magazine twice named him its "Man of the Year."

. . .

Churchill, with whom Marshall had often struggled, readily praised Marshall, calling him the "noblest Roman of them all."

With the strength and courage and vision of the great George Marshall in mind, I am joining with notable leaders to urge all Americans to follow a "new Marshall Plan" for America and its allies. This book will spell out the new rules of patriotic economics – the underpinnings of a new Marshall Plan – again for America's allies, but importantly, also for America itself. Let us now describe the new rules of patriotic economics, so you can act now to secure freedom and prosperity for yourself, your loved ones, and your nation.

The noblest motive
is the public good.
Virgil

And so, my fellow Americans,
ask not what your country can
do for you; ask what you can do
for your country.
President John Fitzgerald
Kennedy, 1961

The New Rules of Patriotic Economics

No act of kindness, no matter how small, is ever wasted.
Aesop, 550BC

Rule GROUND ZERO: *We patriots will continue to give blood and leverage our blood.*

Millions of Americans responded to the Red Cross' appeal for blood immediately following the attacks, often selflessly waiting in long lines at blood donation centers to do their part for their fellow citizens. While it is true that collected blood has a shelf life of only 42 days, the Red Cross has taken steps, including freezing, to ensure that the vast quantities of blood donated in response to the attacks will not be "dumped." Nonetheless, the best thing we can do as patriots is to donate blood again as soon as we are able, and to continue to donate blood on a regular schedule. A statement released by the Red Cross and available on its website (www.redcross.org) said:

> "The United States is moving toward a war footing. These terrorist attacks may not be over and the American Red Cross must ensure an available supply of blood, including a reserve for both civilian and military use, so we are prepared in this period of great uncertainty," said Red Cross spokesperson Lesly Hallman. "The American Red Cross is growing collections by encouraging current donors to give as often as possible, recruiting new blood

donors, leveraging existing freezing and storage technologies as well as rapidly bringing on line new technologies to ensure a sustained and stable American blood supply."

A way to leverage your blood donations is to give platelets. In a process called apheresis, your blood is pumped through a machine that separates out the platelets and then returns the rest of the blood to you. About 18% of your platelets are removed in the two-hour procedure, enough for one platelet transfusion that, for example, an organ or bone marrow transplant patient needs. The beauty of platelet donation is that it takes six whole-blood donations to get the equivalent number of platelets that you donate during one apheresis procedure. Since you can only give whole-blood every eight weeks, it would take you 48 weeks (almost an entire year!) to donate the same number of platelets you can donate right now in only two hours. If you continue to give steadily over an entire year, you can donate slightly more than one platelet transfusion by donating whole-blood, or you can gain leverage 25-fold by donating 26 platelet transfusions by apheresis. Clearly, if you really want to leverage your time and your blood, give platelets!

I call this rule "Rule Ground Zero" in tribute to the heroic rescue workers at Ground Zero in New York City and to the many who gave blood and rose up to support the victims and their families. Giving blood is the way we can most directly benefit all the terrorist victims and our fellow Americans. It is also the easiest. So contact your local Red Cross chapter and give blood again today. You can find more information about donating by calling the Red Cross at 1-800-GIVE LIFE or by visiting www.redcross.org.

Real friendship is shown in times of trouble;
prosperity is full of friends.
Euripides, c. 425BC

Hold a true friend with both your hands.
Nigerian Proverb

RULE 1: *WE PATRIOTS SHOULD VOTE WITH OUR DOLLARS AS WELL AS WITH OUR BALLOTS.*

Without a doubt, all people with the freedom to vote should exercise this right in each and every election they are eligible to participate in. This is a principle of all democracies, in good times or bad.

In the aftermath of the terrorist attacks, I now call on patriots to further exercise their right to vote, but this time, casting their votes with dollars instead of political ballots. By buying US- and allied-produced goods and services, patriots will maximize their own well-being by enhancing the security and prospects of our great nation and our loyal allies.

In Economics 101, we learn that given limited resources (in this case, dollars), we make decisions about allocating those resources (i.e. spending our dollars) so as to maximize our "utility." *What is utility?* In the simplest terms, utility may be seen as happiness. Thus, we spend our hard-earned dollars in ways that will maximize our happiness. In this book, however, patriotic economics goes beyond simple self-centered happiness to define utility as a measure of "satisfaction" or an even deeper "well-being." We achieve satisfaction and maximize well-being as a vital and loyal part of a community and a noble nation.

"International Economics 101," a core of what I teach at Emory University, familiarizes us with the benefits of free trade. Nations produce goods and services where they have a "comparative advantage." When nations specialize in areas of comparative advantage and then trade freely, global consumers end up with more of everything than if each nation tried to produce every good and service for itself. Thus, the United States specializes – produces and exports – where we have a comparative advantage, trading for (i.e. purchasing and importing) the many goods and services from foreign nations who have a comparative advantage (that is, lower relative costs) in their production.

This is a nice bit of explanation for global trade, but what does this have to do with economic patriotism? In the aftermath of the day of infamy, September 11, 2001, I am modifying my personal creed to: I believe in free trade, and I believe in freedom. I will buy goods and services produced in the United States and in those nations who step up now, not only as loyal allies of the United States but of all freedom-loving peoples. News coverage has shown us which nations are strong allies in the fight for civilization. (Clearly, the United Kingdom comes to mind.) Look for products produced in the United States and its allies when you are spending your hard-earned dollars. We should buy US, but we should also buy imported products, whenever *allies* in the fight for freedom have the comparative advantage in their production.

The point of this book is to help readers thrive, while they help their country. If you buy from nations that likely will turn around and buy from the US, you enhance your own job prospects and future income. Beyond favorable news coverage, how else might we identify our trading allies so that we can target our purchases towards them?

Clearly, our NAFTA allies, Canada and Mexico, are our closest trading partners. If we buy Mexican goods, for example, we will end the vicious circle or boomerang effect that has threatened to cripple the economy of our neighbor and its freedom-loving new leader, Vicente Fox. The beauty of NAFTA-partners Canada and Mexico is that *their* citizens often buy US products. So, if our economy grows, they will be able to rapidly increase their purchases of *our* products – just as they were doing before our impending recession curtailed our purchases of their products to such an extent that we were plunging *their* economies into recession, harming *their* ability to buy from their big friend and neighbor – the United States.

Other noble allies such as the United Kingdom, the Netherlands, other nations of the European Union, and Australia also purchase a great deal from the United States, and will enhance their purchases dramatically if the US fights fear and unites to restore economic growth to our own nation and to our allied trading partners.

Our textbook trade theory implies that we do not need to balance bilateral (direct two-sided) trade with each nation. We can buy a lot from a nation if it has a comparative advantage in some product we want, without necessarily having comparative advantage in something that they want. Thus, the US often has large bilateral trade deficits with various nations. However, at a time of national emergency and having already plunged into a recession that calls for a recovery program, such as this new Marshall Plan for America and allies, we should direct our dollars at importing products from trade partner allies who are more likely to send that dollar back by buying US exports, and thus creating jobs for our fellow citizens.

Fortunately, we have reams of trade data at our disposal to help us identify who our trade partner allies are. You can access these data online at many sites (for example, www.bea.doc.gov). Table 1 shows which nations have the biggest shares of our export market. Which nations buy US goods and services? Goods trade, because it comprises both manufactures (e.g. cars) and commodities (e.g. oil, wheat), is much larger than services trade (e.g. tourism, entertainment), so let us focus on it. The table shows that Canada and Mexico are by far, the biggest markets for US exports of goods. Combined, they buy nearly 38% of our goods exports. Japan, the United Kingdom, Germany, and South Korea are also large purchasers of our products. These nations are our clear allies and friends, creating jobs in the US by buying American. Conversely, a number of nations have very miniscule shares of our export market, when compared to the very large number of imports we accept from them.

A number of nations buy a much larger percent or share of our total exports than they sell to us as shares of our total imports. Nations such as Australia, Netherlands, Belgium and Luxembourg are our allies and have created many jobs in the US by demanding American products.

TABLE 1: Our Friends Buy Our Exports

	Share of total US exports (BUY from the US)	Share of total US imports (SELL to the US)
Canada	23.14%	19.08%
Mexico	14.40%	11.17%
Japan	8.31%	11.96%
United Kingdom	5.27%	3.54%
Germany	3.75%	4.78%
South Korea	3.52%	3.29%
Taiwan	3.09%	3.31%
Netherlands	2.81%	0.79%
France	2.62%	2.43%
Singapore	2.28%	1.57%
China	2.09%	8.17%
Brazil	1.98%	1.13%
Hong Kong	1.88%	0.94%
Belgium & Luxembourg	1.85%	0.84%
Australia	1.58%	0.52%
Italy	1.42%	2.04%
Venezuela	0.71%	1.52%

We can clearly see that the US is the "Big Kahuna" of the world's import markets by looking at Figure 1. The US is the world's dominant market, as our imports of goods exceed those of the next three biggest importers combined, or the combined total of the next biggest five after that! This graph clearly shows that the US is the world's major importer of goods, so any nation that wants a piece of this market ought to stand with us now. It is important to note that we are also by far the world's largest importer of services. No one else even comes close. If nations want to create jobs and wealth within their borders by exporting to the dominant US market, they must stand with the alliance for freedom and civilization in the war against terrorism.

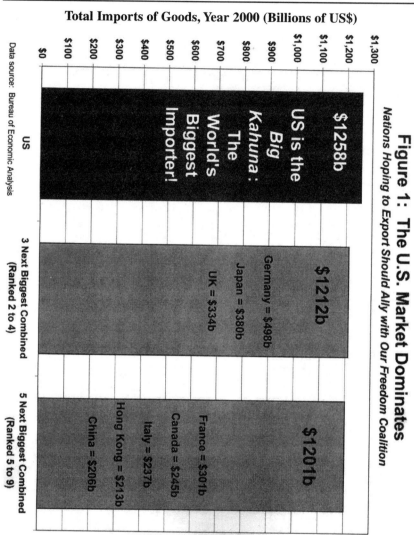

Total Imports of Goods, Year 2000 (Billions of US$)

Figure 1: The U.S. Market Dominates

Nations Hoping to Export Should Ally with Our Freedom Coalition

US: $1258b — US is the Big Kahuna: The World's Biggest Importer!

3 Next Biggest Combined (Ranked 2 to 4): $1212b — Germany = $498b, Japan = $380b, UK = $334b

5 Next Biggest Combined (Ranked 5 to 9): $1201b — France = $301b, Canada = $245b, Italy = $237b, Hong Kong = $213b, China = $206b

Data source: Bureau of Economic Analysis

The US has a mighty economy. We are first in the world ranking by a large magnitude in our exports of goods and of services. However, we are not even close to having export revenues larger than the combined totals of the next biggest two or three export nations. We have provided a locomotive of growth and job creation for other nations in the world via our large, rich, and open import market for their products. Indeed, the US has been swallowing trade deficits of a mammoth $450 billion yearly, much larger than any deficits in world history. We buy a lot more from most nations than we sell to them. Ironically, the gargantuan US trade deficit thus gives us a lot of political leverage: if nations do not want to play ball with us by the rules of justice, freedom, and tolerance, they stand to lose a lot more export sales than we do.

I am proud to live in a nation that is always an engine for global growth, but after September 11, I am observant of who will stand with us in the worldwide battle for prosperity and freedom. So should you be: buy American and allied-made goods and services!

The only thing we have to fear is fear itself.
Franklin Delano Roosevelt, 1933

*There were many dark moments when my faith in
humanity was sorely tested, but I would not and
could not give myself up to despair.*
Nelson Mandela, 1994

RULE 2: *THE ONLY THING WE HAVE TO FEAR IS FEAR ITSELF: OUR FAITH CAN OVERCOME RECESSION AND RESTORE PROSPERITY. CONSUME NOW!*

Consumption is the key to our economic recovery. Individuals' consumption spending is the only thing that kept the US out of a recession into summer 2001, and it is the only thing that can save our economy now.

Let me put into print what I was pronouncing in the days immediately after the shocking terrorist attacks on civilization. The US economy had fallen into a recession BEFORE our commercial planes were turned against us as incendiary missiles. Indeed, on *CNN Headline News*, I proclaimed the Friday *before* the tragic attack that we were likely in recession when we received the report of a jump in the US unemployment figures. At that time, I called for further interest rate cuts, stating they were needed *before* the October 2 Federal Reserve meeting. I was urging such further economic stimulus as early as two weeks before the attacks.

Why were quick and surprisingly strong Federal Reserve cuts of at least 50 basis points (lowering the overnight "Federal funds" interest rate another 0.5%, all the way down to 3%) necessary even before the attack? Government data are reported only after a time lag or delay, and often are revised months and even years after the fact. Although the data did not yet confirm the recession, I knew of far too many executives, workers, farmers, and other people looking for new jobs to believe that we had managed to skirt the much-feared recession. This recession fear was provoked by the "wealth effect" being shoved into reverse by the bursting of the stock market "bubble," shown by the NASDAQ losing two-thirds of its value in barely over a year from its March 10, 2000 peak. It is my claim that the *major* loss we will suffer in our stock market values occurred *prior* to the September 11 atrocity.

Why does this matter to us? We should not give murderous terrorists the satisfaction of thinking they pushed the mighty US economy, the largest and greatest in world history, into a recession! Indeed, I think the patriotic duty and sense of purpose their heinous acts ignited will catalyze our recovery from a recession we had already slid into *before* their violence brought focus to our nation.

Let us take an historical perspective. Since data often get revised, many people have a mistaken view of the US economy during the Gulf War of 1991. We were actually falling into recession before Saddam Hussein sent Iraqi troops into Kuwait. The recession was caused more by the Federal Reserve raising interest rates to forestall an inflation it believed was imminent than by Saddam's troops. The higher interest rates slowed spending and thus production and income generation in the United States, a recessionary impulse that was exacerbated by the insecurity and economic sanctions bred by Operation Desert Shield. It is my contention that the spending power and the end of uncertainty as well as the surge of patriotism unleashed by the successful military efforts of Operation Desert Storm lifted the United States out of recession – a recession that had been caused more by our internal forces, such as the fight against inflation, than by external ones.

Economic data are often substantially revised well after the period reported. For example, try to look for the "double-dip recession" after the Gulf War, a phrase which figured prominently in the 1992 Presidential election campaign. Due to data revisions, it disappeared! I suspect that in a few years, we will look back at the revised second and third quarter data of 2001 and realize that the US economy was already falling into a recession. I also believe that in a few years, we will be able to reflect back and say: "Those unconscionable terrorists inspired a sleeping giant to wake-up – the horrific crimes visited upon innocent civilians galvanized all of us to work together to promote the freedom, security, and tolerance they sought to destroy. Terrorists cannot cripple the US economy and financial markets." Indeed, I hope that as people read this book they will be inspired, as I am, to go out and "buy American" (see Rule 1), and lift our economy out of the recession.

Before economic numbers and reports were rendered insignificant by the loss of innocent human life, the issue we were debating in our nation was: Are consumers falling into such fear of economic insecurity that they will drive the United States into a recession? As discussed above, the last two weeks before the terrorist attacks in New York, Washington, and Pennsylvania were ones where government reports were inspiring me to call for a surprisingly sudden and strong interest rate cut by the Federal Reserve. My point was that the only thing that had kept us out of recession was the confidence of the US consumer. Indeed, growth in consumption spending had kept the US economy afloat while business investment (e.g. on new computers and fiber optics and telecommunications equipment) plunged with the demise of the dot.coms and the bursting of the NASDAQ tech stock price speculative bubble. Thus, consumption spending had increased to *over* two-thirds of the US economy (from exactly two-thirds of US GDP in 1998 to 69% of our nominal GDP at the end of the second quarter of 2001) while business investment spending had declined to below 17% by the end of the second quarter of 2001.

Spending by foreigners on US-made goods and services is another important component of the US economy. But, the increasing strength of our currency was making it ever more difficult for foreigners to purchase our exports. Potential foreign purchasers found their local currency prices of US exports were rising to prohibitive heights due to the strength of the US currency. The strong US dollar was also crippling US farmers and manufacturers – indeed, it reminded me of the mid-1980s, when a too-strong dollar crippled our manufacturing exports and sparked real fears of a "*de*-industrialization of America."

During that earlier "strong dollar" episode, I was working at the Federal Reserve. I would like to applaud our leaders who worked for and accomplished a decline of the US dollar against the key foreign currencies, particularly at the September 1985 G-5 Accord (the central banks of the five big industrial nations) in the Plaza Hotel in New York. It may seem unpatriotic to say that we needed then, and we need now, to push *down* the value of our dollar against such major foreign currencies as the Japanese *yen* and the German *mark* or the *Euro*.

This, however, is the reason we teach Economics 101 or Finance 101, along with this new Patriotic Economics: to educate our citizens that sometimes what seems "right" is not in the best interest of our farmers, our manufacturers, American labor, and our business in general. As we began to discuss above, a strong dollar means production coming from US soil gets too expensive for potential foreign purchasers, crippling our exports.

A look at our declining exports even BEFORE the terrorism confirms my story. The July 2001 U.S export total fell steeply from June, down to $83.7 billion (monthly, seasonally adjusted). Indeed, the June number of $85.9 billion was down from May's figure of $87.6 billion. Compared to the peak achieved the summer before in August 2000 of $91.8 billion, this was indeed quite a drop. These numbers reflect our exports of goods and services. To further illustrate that U.S. manufacturing was clearly in recession BEFORE the terrorist attack, we see that US exports of goods only (not goods AND services) fell to $58.8 billion in July 2001, a steep fall from the $67.4 billion peak value.

Similarly, a too-strong dollar shackles our laborers, businesses, and especially our manufacturers and farmers, by making the price of imports cheaper. Imports of foreign-produced goods and services look less expensive as the dollar strengthens and other currencies weaken. Relative cheapness of imported goods is usually not a sign of dumping, which occurs when foreign firms deliberately sell their products into the US market below their actual costs to drive US production out of business. Rather, the point is that foreigners' actual cost in US dollar terms *does* become lower than the cost of our own production, because our dollar is very costly and their national monies are much less expensive.

Some US government officials, including recent US Treasury Secretaries, have been advocating a "strong US dollar policy." I don't agree with this policy. Certainly, as a patriot, I would not want to see a very weak US dollar – that could cause inflation in the United States, scare away foreign investors who create jobs in the United States, and lead to some instability in our financial system. However, there is a large gulf between a very low or weak US dollar, which would diminish our international standing, and a too-strong dollar, which puts heavy ankle-weights on our workers in what should be a fair and free market race with foreign competitors. All patriots should advocate for our workers being allowed to run this race without heavy ankle-weights, that is, without undue government restrictions and barriers and the massive load of a too-costly US dollar.

Let me return to the main point. We have so far discussed three of the four sectors that drive demand for US goods and services: consumer spending, business investment, and foreign purchases of our exports. In the

United States, pre-September 11, 2001, exports were already declining due to the strong US$. As we discussed a few pages ago, investment spending was also declining. So, consumption spending seemed to be the only engine of growth for the US economy. What about the fourth sector? Was that growing and demanding more US goods and services?

The fourth sector is government purchases, and as you probably guessed, growth here has been decelerating for awhile, ever since the elder George Bush administration. The end of the Cold War was truly a remarkable event in world history along with the (almost unthinkable a decade or two ago) emergence of Russia as a potential ally, not a mortal foe. This massive change in the world's superpower structure led to the radical downsizing of US military and intelligence capabilities. The US economy and many Americans gained economically from the resultant "peace dividend." Clearly, eliminating waste and inefficiency in government spending, including fat that was clearly in our military budget during the years of the Cold War, is a good and necessary thing. However, when the going gets tough, freedom-seeking citizens not only in the United States, but also throughout the world, always turn to the US military. Now, when we need them the most, many of our most patriotic officers, including former leaders of the US Rangers and our Special Operations and Delta Forces, are working in civilian clothes, having been downsized in a manner reminiscent of the layoffs at Lucent, our "Big 3" automakers, and now aviation-related industries.

I do not exaggerate the extent of retrenched spending our military has suffered. According to the Congressional Budget Office (data available online at www.cbo.gov), defense spending amounted to over 6% of GDP in 1985 - 87, but only 3.0% in 1999 and 2000. This is a huge relative decline, totaling more than half of the share of our nation's income that we devote to defending the security and freedom of our diverse residents. The US has assembled the bravest and the most advanced fighting force the world has ever known. Did we hamstring our own protectors, the US military and intelligence agencies, with these massive defense cuts?

Thus, of the four possible areas of increased demand for US production, only the consumer sector was keeping our economy afloat. Firms had cut back on new plant and equipment spending following the NASDAQ bust, so investment spending declined as a share of our economy and even in absolute terms. Government spending was also decelerating. The increased trade deficit resulting in part from US exports looking too expensive to other nations due to our strong dollar, indicated that purchases by foreigners was not a sector of growth either. I have included the numbers below in Table 2 so you can see it for yourself.

The last two lines tell the tale: US GDP excluding consumption in real or inflation-adjusted terms actually declined somewhat significantly in the year up to the last quarter before the attack. To put it another way, the year-to-year growth to the end of Q2-2001 of $112.3 billion in real GDP was far more than 100% accounted for by the growth of consumer spending. Consumption grew nearly

Table 2a: Consumer Spending Boomed, Rising to Over 2/3 of GDP

(Nominal GDP and its components, 2000Q2 to 2001Q2)

	2000-Q2	2000-Q3	2000-Q4	2001-Q1	2001-Q2
Nominal GDP	9857.6	9937.5	10027.9	10141.7	10202.6
Consumption	6674.9	6785.5	6871.4	6977.6	7044.6
as a % of GDP	67.7%	68.3%	68.5%	68.8%	69.0%
Investment	1792.4	1788.4	1780.3	1722.8	1669.9
as a % of GDP	18.2%	18.0%	17.8%	17.0%	16.4%
Net exports	-350.8	-380.6	-390.6	-363.8	-347.4
as a % of GDP	-3.6%	-3.8%	-3.9%	-3.6%	-3.4%
Government	1577.2	1570	1582.8	1603.4	1625
as a % of GDP	16.0%	15.8%	15.8%	15.8%	15.9%

Table 2b: Only Consumption Was Rising, The Rest of GDP Was Already

Declining During the Year Before the September 11 Attack

(Real GDP and Consumption, 2000Q2 to 2001Q2)

	2000-Q2	2000-Q3	2000-Q4	2001-Q1	2001-Q2
Real GDP	9229.4	9260.1	9303.9	9334.5	9341.7
Consumption (real)	6226.3	6292.1	6341.1	6388.5	6428.4
Real GDP minus Real Consumption	3003.1	2968.0	2962.8	2946.0	2913.3

twice as fast as overall GDP, meaning that consumption offset declines in the other components and grew fast enough to drag the whole economy forward.

But even this largest component of demand seemed poised to take a plunge before the September 11 attack, as consumer confidence was falling along with our employment prospects and our NASDAQ stock portfolios. Economic reports coming out the week before September 11 were indeed discouraging, and I feared, would cause consumers to curtail spending. The unemployment rate was rising rapidly, as shown by the report on September 7, where unemployment jumped from 4.5% to 4.9%. Further, my research showed that the unemployment rate would be much higher if we added back in potential workers who were too discouraged by frequent rejection of their job applications to be actively searching for work. Thus, because they were not actively searching in the week of the unemployment survey, these "discouraged workers" were not counted as part of the labor force and thus were not counted as unemployed. Surely, many of these discouraged workers would accept a job if offered. If we count their unemployed status as "hidden unemployment," we see that the unemployment rate really increased much more rapidly than the official reported rate. Indeed, I believe unemployment was actually over 6.0%, rather than the reported 4.9%, because of additional discouraged workers or hidden unemployed.

By September 11, layoffs were accumulating rapidly, as were losses in the stock market, and we had weekly reports of near-record levels of new claims for unemployment insurance. Clearly, the ground had already been set for a strong decline in consumer confidence and we pundits were already saying: the US is already in a recession, because the only thing that was holding our economy up was consumption spending. Indeed, economic reports covering the period following the attacks have been released, and not surprisingly, showed a discernible drop in consumer confidence. But consider this in a deeper perspective. Figure 2 shows the movement in consumer confidence as measured by the University of Michigan Consumer Sentiment Survey. Note we cannot escape the conclusion that the uncertainty and anguish caused by the terrible acts of September 11 exacerbated an already declining trend in US consumer confidence, but the trend began much earlier. Finally, there is still a significant level of confidence shown.

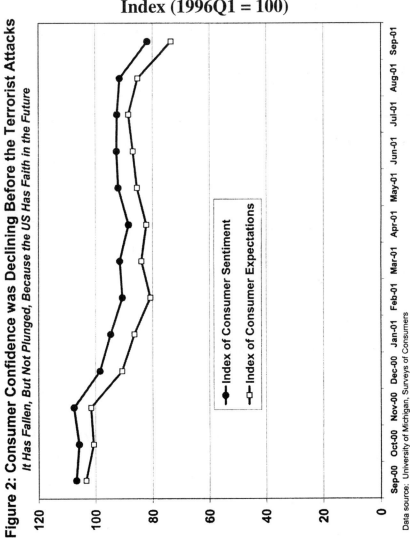

Figure 2: Consumer Confidence was Declining Before the Terrorist Attacks
It Has Fallen, But Not Plunged, Because the US Has Faith in the Future

Index (1996Q1 = 100)

Data source: University of Michigan, Surveys of Consumers

Now, our economy's health depends on our decisions. We stand ready to ignite a *vicious* or a *virtuous* circle, as depicted in Figure 3. Will we boost our spending and return our economy to growth and health, or will we succumb to fear and bad news? If we succumb to fear for our future, we play right into the hands of terrorists by staying home and curtailing our consumption of US products. If we succumb to fear, we allow terrorists to catalyze a plunging of our consumption spending into a deep recession. That is why I echo the words Franklin Delano Roosevelt spoke in 1933 to give heart to another generation that faced uncertain times: "The only thing we have to fear is fear itself." We hold in our own hands the future of the economy. Whichever path we choose now becomes a self-fulfilling prophecy. Choose to spend and feel confident in our futures, and the economy will rebound and reward us with even greater confidence. Choose to succumb to fear and further curtail spending, and the economy will dip into recession and lead to only greater fear and losses of confidence.

I have chosen to pursue the virtuous self-fulfilling prophecy, and so should you. As I speak to fellow citizens at various conferences and classes, I see Americans rallying to banish fear and turn the terrorists' horrific crimes into a patriotic passion that will motivate us to purchase the many important products supplied by the United States and its allies. Let me give you one example. I kept appearing on television with shorter hair nearly each day in the week after the World Trade Center attack. My local barber had told me there were almost no customers coming in. My barber has a mortgage to meet – so does

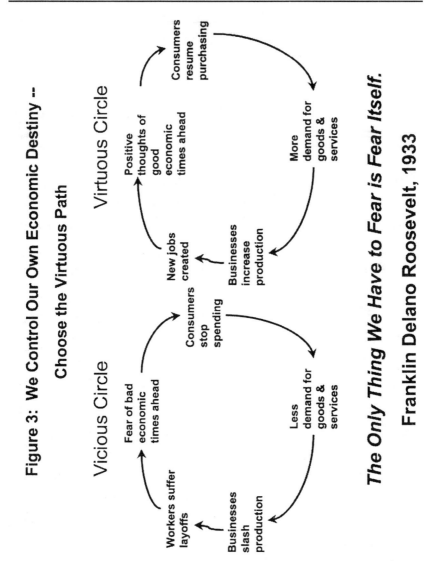

Figure 3: We Control Our Own Economic Destiny -- Choose the Virtuous Path

The Only Thing We Have to Fear is Fear Itself.

Franklin Delano Roosevelt, 1933

your barber or hair stylist. Please put down this book and go get a haircut – whether you need one or not! Go to stores, especially of retailers who supported the rescue efforts, and buy not just American flags, but American or ally-made American flags. I can shine my own shoes and carry my own bag, however, please join me in getting your shoes shined and your bags carried every chance you have. These entrepreneurs are trying to live the American dream, but they must keep paying rent for their shoeshine stands in airports and hotels, and now they are really hurting.

Show your patriotism with your dollars, especially if you are financially secure. Go to a local retailer and buy whatever products you can afford and can use – after reading the labels very carefully. Do not let the names or brands fool you – if someone calls themselves the "All American Toy Company," you can be pretty sure that they are trying to hide the fact that they may not be creating jobs in the United States and our allies. Check labels, ask questions, and then spend for America's future.

Again, I must emphasize that my plan may seem to go against my ivory tower academic training to advocate free trade regardless of political and social reasons. At least until freedom and tolerance clearly have the upper hand, and freedom-loving citizens of all religions, races, and preferences are more secure on a global basis, I will be buying foreign-made products based on two principles. I will buy from nations who have a "comparative advantage" in producing particular products AND who stand with the United States as allies in the moral war for freedom, security, and tolerance.

We can control our own destiny. If we fear terrorists, or do not have faith in the future growth and stability of the US economy, we will stay home and bring a deep recession upon ourselves. To succumb to fear rather than to rally to the fight for freedom and prosperity allows terrorists to gain satisfaction that their evil deeds caused us to fall into a gloom and doom of a psychological depression that would lead to an economic depression or at least a severe recession. Keep in mind that the United States has not seen an economic depression since the 1930s.

Instead, let us turn the patriotic fervor that unites us into action after so many were killed in the World Trade Center, the Pentagon, and on the fields of Pennsylvania. Rise up and banish the fear that was leading our consumer confidence to plunge, pulling our nation into a recession even BEFORE the terrorists revealed our deep unity.

Never underestimate the power of the human spirit and the ability we each have to control our own minds and think positive thoughts even in the most adverse circumstances. I need only cite Nelson Mandela as an example. Mandela was jailed for 27 years. He faced physical deprivation and tremendous hardship and cruelty. However, his jailers could never control his spirit or his noble mind. They could do hateful acts, but they could not make him respond in the same way. Indeed, many of his jailers now admit that his nobility and spiritual force moved them to admire him greatly and even to befriend him covertly during his physical captivity. They soon realized they could capture his body, but neither his consciousness nor his spirit were subject to control by terrorists or bigots. This is the power of a tolerant and freedom-loving mind. Nelson Mandela's autobiography, *Long Walk to Freedom*, is an inspirational work that I urge every person to read.

Mandela's partner in striving to bring about truth and reconciliation in South Africa was Archbishop Desmond

Tutu. At Emory University, we were blessed with the presence of Archbishop Tutu for a couple of years when he accepted an opportunity we offered him to write and reflect after his arduous and successful struggle, along with so many other brave South Africans, against the evils of apartheid, and then against the evils of a blanket revenge. We learned so much from the Archbishop. He taught us about reconciliation, the power of the human spirit, and the value of seeking a reasoned approach to find justice, security, and ultimately a world order that preempts attacks on innocent and freedom-loving peoples, no matter their religion, race, or personal preferences.

If Mandela could control his destiny while jailed by an evil regime, can we not take the small step to control our own destiny by getting off the couch and going to our local stores? We do not have to give in to jailers or captors or terrorists. We can turn the vicious attacks into a call for action. If we banish fear and follow Rule 1, we will re-ignite what were the slumbering economies of the United States and its allies.

The consumer sector is so dominant in our economy that a drop-off in its spending could plunge the world into recession. Now, I call upon all citizens with secure jobs or financial means to follow Rule 2 of Patriotic Economics, and lift the economy through purchases.

The purpose of this book is to show that we can thrive individually by following the action plan herein, while helping those less fortunate by contributing to an upturn in the global economy. Now is the time to benefit personally by finding great bargains on purchases, such as a new house, car, furniture, clothing, etc. If you have some purchasing power, you can thrive by taking advantage of bargain prices and record-low interest rates now available. At the same time you are gaining, cumulative actions such as these will create jobs for those less fortunate.

Government is a trust, and the officers of the government are trustees; and both the trust and the trustees are created for the benefit of the people.

Henry Clay, 1829

RULE 3: WE CAN TRUST OUR INDEPENDENT FEDERAL RESERVE SYSTEM: IT FIGHTS FOR OUR FINANCIAL FREEDOM AND SECURITY.

I was working at the Federal Reserve during the historic stock market crash of Monday, October 19, 1987, and I will always remember Chairman Alan Greenspan coming out to address the world. He said that the Fed stood ready to provide any and all liquidity needed to forestall a panic or a crash that could devastate the entire financial system and threaten the financial freedom of US citizens and our allies. In Finance 101, we teach that "providing liquidity" is a euphemism, i.e. a nice way to say "we'll print money and provide it as reserves to the banking system before we will let the savings of hardworking Americans be threatened." By standing strong and suggesting that, if needed, we can replenish the cash reserves in the banking system, the Federal Reserve usually can forestall panic. The beauty is that a strong leader, by stating that we have printing presses for money and will use them if needed to fight the forces of chaos and panic, can usually inspire the citizens of this patriotic nation to relax. We barely have to turn on the US printing presses to find a stable anchor for our financial system without incurring the potential inflationary costs of a massive printing of dollars.

The Greenspan-led Federal Reserve acted brilliantly and patriotically once again in the current tragic circumstances. Following the terrorist attacks, the Federal Reserve brilliantly orchestrated moves among the central banks of all our allies. These moves were not secret – and the strategy worked perfectly. The central banks showed that they were awake, aware, and ready to provide whatever reserves were needed to ensure the safety and soundness of our financial system. Their words were matched by actions. All of us "Fed watchers" could see that the Federal Reserve and others such as the European Central Bank were taking actions to add monetary reserves or "liquidity" into the free world's banking system. Their moves were so clear, so strong, and so timely that I and other independent-minded commentators were able to report with the greatest of integrity and credibility that our concern was for the fate of potential victims and their families, and for the brave rescue workers – there was just no possibility of a systemic risk to the financial system.

My time at the Federal Reserve taught me two things about the system. First, you'd better get up real early if you want to get up before the hardworking central bankers. Second, I learned a great deal about character and the importance of always avoiding conflicts of interest, from the integrity that is a hallmark of the US Federal Reserve System. No one within the Federal Reserve System would ever compromise the basic integrity and independence of the world's leading financial institution. The honorable thing to do if you have any penchant for "playing the markets" is to resign. I admire and respect my patriotic friends within the System.

You can trust your Federal Reserve System, the lynchpin of our entire financial system. The fact that the Fed cut interest rates to a level not seen in 40 years within three weeks of the September 11 attack shows that these public servants stand ready to provide whatever liquidity is needed to keep our economic and financial system healthy. We can thrive as individuals if we take advantage of the record-low interest rates (see Rule 6).

Order marches with weighty and measured strides;
disorder is always in a hurry.
Napolean Bonaparte, 1804 –15

The mob has many heads but no brains.
Thomas Fuller, 1732

RULE 4: *WE WERE CORRECT TO CLOSE THE EXCHANGES IN NEW YORK; BUT MARKETS NEVER SLEEP — WHEN YOU HEAR BAD NEWS, IT IS OFTEN TOO LATE TO SELL.*

We all need to understand the nature of today's 24-hour worldwide stock market. Today, we "pass the book" (a trading firm's set of open accounts or buy-and-sell orders) around with the sun, as international exchanges open and close around the world, no longer confined to 9:30AM to 4:00PM Eastern Standard Time. Even within the US, we have 24/7 electronic trading. Now that we live in the networked economy, stock trading occurs not just in Manhattan, nor only in formal, organized physically located stock exchanges in the US and around the world. We have Instinet, for example.

It is also important to understand that markets, or particular stocks, do not have to open at prices where they last closed. Indeed, news often causes them to "gap down" at the open. This is based on supply and demand: after bad news, when the particular stock or the whole market reopens, there may not be very much demand to buy. If you then think that you're going to sell on the bad news, you just end up being one more of those who are adding to supply, exacerbating the situation of great supply and very little demand. The auctioneer or the market-maker (or the invisible hand of the market) can only fill your sell order by finding a very low price that attracts some bottom fishers to demand the shares that you and others want to supply. Thus, you may end up selling to opportunists at such a low price that you satisfy their bottom-fishing, profit-seeking motives, but you did so by giving up your own claims to a great company at the worst possible moment.

The key is to hang on to your stocks and mutual funds, as the market has already reacted to the bad news well before you have a chance to sell. You only end up losing big time by selling into a down market. The wisdom of not "selling America short" was made clear by the fact that all US stock markets were significantly higher the Friday after we began military operations with our British allies, than they were right after the NYSE reopened on September 17. Again, actions taken to thrive individually also helped our nation and its businesses.

Patience and diligence, like faith, remove mountains.
William Penn, 1693

Whoever has no patience has no wisdom.
Sa'di, 1258

RULE 5: *WE CAN SECURE OUR OWN AND OUR LOVED ONES' FINANCIAL FREEDOM BY STEADILY INVESTING IN STOCKS OR MUTUAL FUNDS FOR THE LONG RUN.*

This is a corollary rule to the one we just discussed. Beyond not selling stocks and mutual funds at this point, we can secure financial freedom for ourselves and our loved ones by stepping up our equity investing.

Table 3 contains a list of the companies from the S&P100 that were down, during the week the New York Stock Exchange reopened, more than 50% from their peak prices over the last two years. Coincidentally, exactly 50% of this prestigious list of 100 globally-recognized firms were down over 50%, so surely there are great buying opportunities out there! Prices change while books sit on shelves, so I urge each of you to do your own homework. Patience will be rewarded.

If you are hesitant to pick individual stocks, now is a great time to invest in mutual funds. By far, the best way to invest in mutual funds is to have a certain dollar amount deducted from your checking account or paycheck each month. Many mutual funds will let you invest as little as

Table 3: 50 of the S&P100 firms were selling at less than 50% of their peak price

Company Name	% Decline	Company Name	% Decline
1 Aes Corporation	-69.8	26 Honeywell Intl	-67.7
2 Allegheny Tech.	-51.1	27 Intel Corp	-75.0
3 American Express Co	-61.6	28 JP Morgan Chase & Co	-56.8
4 AOL Time Warner	-71.4	29 Limited Inc (The)	-66.2
5 At&T Corp	-65.8	30 Lucent Technologies	-93.8
6 Bank One Corp	-57.5	31 Medimmune Inc	-65.7
7 Black & Decker Corp	-55.3	32 Merrill Lynch & Co	-58.1
8 Boeing Co	-61.1	33 Microsoft Corp	-60.4
9 Campbell Soup Co	-53.2	34 Morgan Stanley Dean	-67.5
10 Cisco Systems Inc	-85.5	35 National Semiconduct.	-75.4
11 Clear Channel Comm	-63.1	36 Nextel Communication	-89.9
12 Computer Sciences Co	-69.0	37 Norfolk Southern	-63.2
13 Delta Air Lines Inc	-72.2	38 Nortel Networks	-94.7
14 Dupont	-56.6	39 Oracle Corporation	-78.1
15 Eastman Kodak Co	-61.7	40 Radioshack Corp	-74.7
16 Emc Corp	-90.5	41 Raytheon Co	-61.3
17 Enron Corp	-71.9	42 Rockwell Automation	-50.5
18 Ford Motor Co	-62.1	43 Schlumberger Ltd	-52.5
19 General Electric Co	-53.1	44 Texas Instruments	-79.9
20 General Motors Corp	-58.6	45 Unisys Corp	-83.9
21 Gillette Company	-59.6	46 United Technologies	-54.2
22 Global Crossing Ltd	-95.6	47 Viacom Inc Non-Vot B	-62.8
23 Halliburton Co	-63.4	48 Walt Disney Co	-64.7
24 Hewlett-Packard Co	-81.9	49 Williams Companies	-53.5
25 Home Depot Inc	-57.1	50 Xerox Corp	-90.1

$25 or $50 a month. Steadily investing on a monthly basis in an equity mutual fund allows you to take advantage of *dollar-cost averaging*. Dollar-cost averaging is especially advantageous in volatile times, because steady purchasing allows you to lower your average cost per share. In other words, as the market turns down, your monthly purchases occur at a lower price per share. Instead of just sitting on a stock or mutual fund that has dropped in value, if you purchase more, then ultimately if you go to sell when the stock rises, you will have a lower average cost and thus a higher gain.

Of course, one should never "throw good money after bad" by further purchasing shares of stocks that are likely never to recover. On the other hand, Figure 4 illustrates the value of steady investing. It shows the average annualized growth rate of the NASDAQ from 1991 to the end of 2001. Where will NASDAQ end 2001? We don't know, but I have shown you two possible scenarios. If NASDAQ ends 2001 at 1800, then steady investors who stayed in the market for the whole time will have achieved an annual return of 15.6%. Even if NASDAQ ends at 1500, the annual return since 1991 is still an impressive 13.5%.

The alternatives to putting a share of your income each month into mutual funds and leaving it there as a long-term investment are just not very attractive at this historic moment. Rates available if we put our money in the bank, even if we lock-up our money in certificates of deposit, are too low to fund our retirement or our dependents' college funds at the needed levels.

Indeed, interest rates on bank CDs and shorter-term Treasury bonds have been roughly cut in half since a year ago, as banks have little choice but to follow the Federal Reserve interest rate cuts including the recent half-point cuts on September 17 and on October 2, 2001.

Of course, investing in stocks is never a sure thing. Since the NASDAQ peak of March 10, 2000, the stock market and particularly the tech stocks have taken a severe beating. The year-and-a-half following the March 10, 2000 peak brought a severe bust, a "burst bubble" in the NASDAQ. However, the point of Figure 4 is that, in spite of the decline, if you were investing in stocks for the long-run, you still are doing better than if you squirreled your retirement funds in the bank or in bonds. My first live

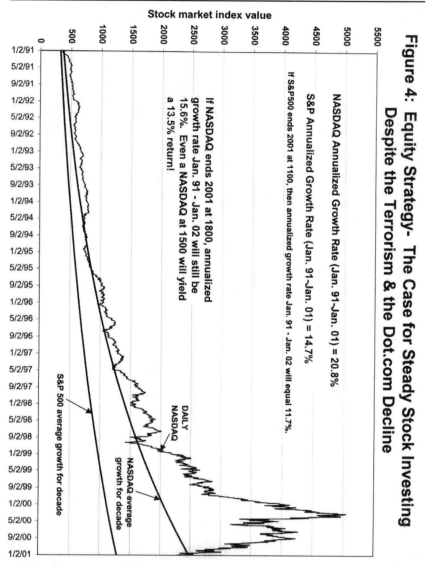

Figure 4: Equity Strategy- The Case for Steady Stock Investing Despite the Terrorism & the Dot.com Decline

appearance on CNN was a few hours before the Gulf War started on January 16, 1991. My basic message was to not delay, as this is the buying opportunity of the decade. Our military will prevail and stocks will soar.

Was this good advice? A mere one decade later, the NASDAQ showed what a great buying opportunity it was:

it went from 400 on January 16, 1991 to 2600 on January 16, 2001. This is a cumulative average growth rate of 21.8% per year, an amazingly high return, especially when we consider that this period includes most of the crash that occurred after the March 10, 2000 peak. This annual growth rate sure beats the current bank or bond interest rates available! I must concede that NASDAQ, and stocks in general, have fallen even further since the 2001 tenth anniversary of the start of the Gulf War. However, even if NASDAQ is only 1600 on January 16, 2002, the eleven-year cumulative average growth rate equals a fine return of 14.4% per year. Clearly, this return dominates any rate you could have gotten at any bank or with any bond.

Of course, the past may not be prologue to the future. However, any patriot knows that the United States is rebuilding. The impressive actions we are taking will lead to economic recovery, helping underpin a volatile but ultimately rising US stock market during the decade to come. Fortunately, US demographic patterns position us perfectly for another good decade for US stock market investors. The entire baby boom, nearly 80 million strong when we include hardworking immigrants who have supplemented our ranks, knows we must save and invest, often in stock mutual funds, if we are to grow retirement funds or college funds enough to secure our own futures.

Selling America short is not only unpatriotic, but it is not the path to a sustainable personal profit. Invest in stock mutual funds and companies with consistently strong global brands, every month, and look back in five years. You will be glad you stood up for America and did not let fear hamstring your future prosperity.

Timeliness is best in all matters.
Hesiod, 8th century BC

RULE 6: *WE PATRIOTS CAN "BUY AMERICAN," DESPITE HAVING LIMITED CASH, BY GAINING FROM RECORD-LOW INTEREST RATES.*

American car manufacturers gave great sums of money and support to the relief effort in New York. Now the car manufacturers and dealers need our support. Our fellow Americans working in all sectors of the auto industry have been facing large layoffs due to falling sales. Go to your local dealer and choose a car that has most of its components made in the United States and/or its allies. (Recall that along with the US "Big Three," many Hondas and Toyotas for example are to some extent American-made. In fact, of all the manufacturing plants in Ohio, the one that employs the most US workers is the Honda plant.) You'll probably be able to get a vehicle at 0% financing, or at least with some of the lowest interest rates you have ever seen for a car, even with a full 5-year financing plan. In addition, there are large cash rebates, no cost optional equipment, and other "freebies" available to further motivate you.

One suggestion you may consider is to accept a large cash rebate instead of favorable financing. Then, use the equity in your home to pay for your new car with cash. Do not follow this strategy unless price gains over the years give you a nice margin of home equity. But if you have the home equity, realize that loans against a home, including a home equity loan, are tax deductible whereas interest on cars, furniture, other consumer items, and credit cards are often financial suicide. I make such a strong statement because you can get hurt twice: paying a high interest rate that is not even tax deductible. Of course, if you do not have cash or equity to tap, you do not have to worry about the tax deductibility of a zero interest loan on your new car!

Marjorie Blanchard gave me a great suggestion: if you are secure financially, buy yourself a new car and donate the car you have been driving to someone less fortunate, perhaps someone who needs it to find, and commute to, a new job. You might also consider donating it to a worthy charity. Help others thrive, while enjoying a new ride at a great price.

If you have a secure job, think about buying a house, or at least refinancing your mortgage or tapping into a home equity loan. Lower rates provide you with extra cash each month to "buy American." Right now, you will find some of the lowest interest rates ever available on, for instance, 15-year mortgages and home equity lines of credit.

Particularly low interest rates are available on mortgages that are fixed for a shorter time, such as 3 or 5 or 7 years before they float. Such adjustable-rate mortgages start with amazingly low interest rates, and with features such as annual and lifetime caps, you can protect yourself in case interest rates spike up in the future. Even after we began military operations the week of October 7, I found numerous rates available on a 3-year or a 5-year ARM below 5% with fairly low closing costs. Indeed, I found a 3.5% rate on a 3-year ARM, but of course, that implied paying some points.

You may be reading this many weeks or months after the beginning of October, so I encourage you to visit bankrate.com, which is the site I use to monitor rates. ARM loans are especially attractive if you know you will be in your new home for a period of years less than the number of years the loan is fixed. These days, many people know at the time of purchase, or refinance, that they likely will be in a particular house for under 5 years, for example, because they plan on moving to a new city for career or retirement reasons or because they plan on buying a more expensive home as their income/wealth increases. They may also plan to upsize or downsize their home choice as their family evolves (e.g. empty nesters). By opting for the 3-, 5-, or 7-year ARM, they can take advantage of an even lower interest rate (and thus a much lower monthly payment) than a 15- or 30-year fixed, and never have to think about the adjustable, post-fixed rate period of the loan.

So please check for yourselves – you may be able to get a balloon loan or one that gets paid back over a full 30 years, while having an amazingly low monthly payment, fixed for the next 3, 5, or 7 years. This may allow you to tap some equity in your home to pay off higher interest rate debt, to take the huge cash incentives to buy a new car without car financing, or to implement a strategy of dollar-cost averaging into stock mutual funds as we describe in this book. This is practical advice that is also patriotic.

The interest rates on mortgages are so attractive right now that even if you refinanced your 30-year mortgage in the year before the attack, you really need to run the numbers to see if it pays to refinance again. Of course, running the numbers will include looking at closing costs and discount points of the new loan, if applicable. Do not include closing costs of your original loan though, as these are what we call in finance, "sunk costs" that should not impact your present decision.

Table 4: Refinance to financial freedom, 15 years early?

15-year vs. 30-year mortgages

	Fifteen Year	Thirty Year	Thirty Year	Thirty Year
Principal:	$100,000	$100,000	$100,000	$100,000
Term (# of Payments):	180	360	360	360
Interest Rate:	5.5%	7.5%	8.5%	9.5%
Monthly Mortgage Payments:	$817.08	$699.21	$768.91	$840.85
Total Payments (over full life of loan)	$147,075	$251,717	$276,809	$302,708
Total Payments Saved if refinanced to a 15 Year Fixed		$104,642	$129,734	$155,632
Present Value of total payments (@ 5% discount rate)	$103,324	$130,251	$143,234	$156,636

Into the second half of October, after two strong Fed interest-cuts, a 15-year fixed mortgage could be had for an astoundingly low, but commonly available, 5.5%. Using this 5.5% rate, I have made Table 4 to show the cost savings of switching your higher rate 30-year fixed mortgage to a lower rate 15-year fixed.

In the extreme case, if your 30-year mortgage has a 9.5% interest rate, not only can you lower your monthly payment by refinancing into a 15-year fixed, you can own your home free and clear much earlier if you adopt the accelerated payment strategy of the 15-year loan. Even at 8.5% on your 30-year fixed, for less than $50 a month more, you get full ownership of your home that much more quickly.

The second and third lines of data in Table 4 tell the tale. You can save a tremendous amount of total payment dollars if you get a 15-year mortgage on your new home or refinance into a 15-year loan if you currently have a 30-year mortgage at a fixed rate over 7% or so. The dollar savings are huge if you have a fairly high 30-year rate now and / or if your mortgage is greater than the $100,000 loan I use in this example.

The last line in the table above also makes an important point, one that I am compelled to clarify as I am a professor of finance. The *present value* of your total payments does not show such a huge divergence from the 15 year to the 30 year as the actual nominal payments. That is, much higher total payments in the 30-year mortgages have a present value that is not nearly so high, because unlike the 15-year mortgage, some of the payments in the 30-year mortgages will be made in the distant future where we cannot be very certain of the actual purchasing power of the dollars you are contracting to pay each month for 360 months. Still, I think it should be clear that you can save 15 years of large payments in nominal terms, while barely paying more per month now, if you refinance now to a 15-

year fixed, especially if you are holding one of the higher rate 30-year mortgages.

Why is the 15-year fixed rate so attractive now? Uncertainty prevails, and a fear of a move into government deficits is a reality. Indeed, I explain in this book why we right now NEED to run government deficits as we win a war against terrorism and against economic recession. This means that many lenders or savers fear locking-in their savings for very long periods, in case we return to inflationary times. Thus, savers have been buying treasury securities that mature in less than 10 years. This has pushed up the price of those shorter-duration notes and bonds, and pushed down the interest rate in the market. So, banks and other lenders can turn around and make attractive deals available for those looking for a 15-year mortgage, or better yet, a 3-, 5-, or 7-year ARM. Lenders think twice, as do savers, before they commit to such a long maturity as a 30-year loan.

Bottom line for you: if you know you will move in a few years, refinance to a very low rate ARM. If you are unsure or if you know you will stay put, a 15-year fixed is probably the answer for you. But if you can get reasonable caps on an ARM, this may be the route to go regardless of your plans to move or stay put.

It is very important that you avoid credit card loans or other high interest loans, particularly since they are not even deductible from your taxes. By contrast, borrowing against your house is tax deductible and is available now at historically low interest rates. These low interest rates are available because we are in a crisis and the Federal

Reserve System has reacted by providing tons of liquidity to the banking system. Also, many people cautious about equity investing have put their money into the bank or into short-term treasuries. This has also driven down short- to medium-term interest rates to all-time lows. Thus, now is a great time to borrow. The US economy will roar again and when it does, interest rates will go up. This is because businesses will want to borrow more to invest in new factories and equipment, and investors will withdraw their savings from their current safe havens (banks and treasury securities) to put their money to work more aggressively in the stock market, in real estate, and in new businesses.

The Federal Reserve made its eighth interest rate cut in a row just before the markets reopened following the terrorist attacks, but this rate cut was needed anyway as we were already in recession. The Fed then made a ninth cut on Oct. 2. I'm still predicting the Fed will make more cuts if needed to get our economy growing again. We have a resolve to rebuild our economy and come back stronger than ever. If you think it's impossible for the Federal Reserve to keep going until they have achieved even 10 or 11 interest rate cuts, let me point out that my research shows that the Greenspan-led Federal Reserve cut rates 25 separate times during the first George Bush administration!

War is an unmitigated evil.
But it certainly does one good thing.
It drives away fear and brings bravery to the surface.
Mohandas K. Gandhi, 1948

In the final choice, a soldier's pack is not so heavy
as a prisoner's chains.
Dwight D. Eisenhower, 1953

RULE 7: *DON'T WORRY ABOUT DEFICIT SPENDING BY OUR GOVERNMENT RIGHT NOW. WHEN AT WAR, A GOVERNMENT DEFICIT CAN* **HELP.**

We must act strongly and swiftly to get the US economy going. We have already discussed the need for consumers to keep spending to fuel a recovery from recession. In fact, we also need our government to spend more to get our economy growing and to create jobs. Emergency government spending is needed, for example, to rebuild sections of our great cities, support industries specifically suffering from the terrorist attacks, heighten security at our airports and borders, and win a worldwide war along with our allies against terrorism. Targeted tax cuts to spur job creation and to put additional money into the pockets of workers are also needed. All this additional federal spending, combined with tax cuts, must dry up the government surplus of the past few years and drive the government to deficits again.

Is not a deficit dangerous? I for one have railed against the accumulation of large deficits into massive government debt (for example, see my first book, *Winning the Global Game*). The point here is that we must look at the overall system and take a longer-term perspective. We can and must get back to government surpluses. However, the time for that will be when the war against terrorism and recession is won. The actions taken now will no doubt exacerbate a growing deficit, but they will also return us to economic growth and prosperity. We can balance our budget again in the future, if we work to create jobs now that will lead to higher income tax revenues for the government. We also need to create enough economic growth so that firms will prosper and profit and thereby pay more corporate taxes to the government, and individuals can once again pay capital gains taxes on their stocks rather than deducting capital losses as so many will do this year.

History teaches us that the mobilization for World War II finally pulled the US economy out of the Great Depression. The times of crises are special times. Such times call for increased government spending and reduced taxes, as well as the vision to see that such short-term government-deficit-producing actions will fuel an economic recovery and hence surpluses down the road. This is also the history of the glorious triumph of the US and its many allies in the 1991 Gulf War.

Tolerance implies no lack of commitment to one's own beliefs. Rather it condemns the oppression or persecution of others.

John F. Kennedy, 1960

RULE 8: *WE MUST BE SELECTIVE AND SECURE AT ALL US BORDERS, BUT NEVER CLOSE THEM. TALENTED, HARDWORKING FREEDOM SEEKERS ARE WELCOME IN THE UNITED STATES, CANADA, AND AUSTRALIA.*

Immigrants are a vital source of vigor and growth in a nation. We must not allow terrorists to close our minds and our national borders to the hardworking immigrants so crucial to our economy.

The United States, Canada, and Australia are far more accepting of immigrants than other nations of the world. How do we know? These three allies rank among the highest in the world in terms of rates of annual in-migration, both in absolute numbers and as a percent of total population. In addition, all three represent some of the highest standards of living or overall human and economic development of any *large* nations on Earth.

Each year, the United Nations issues its *Human Development Report*, which ranks the nations of the world according to a Human Development Index (HDI). The index comprises three major components: longevity (life expectancy), educational attainment (adult literacy and school enrollment ratios), and standard of living, as measured by real GDP per capita (using PPP exchange rates). Following an amazing six year run in first place, Canada was narrowly edged out of the top spot to finish an impressive third in the 2001 report. Australia grabbed the number two spot, while the United States finished 6th overall. (You can access the UNDP's 2001 *Human Development Report* for free at www.undp.org/hdr2001/.)

This correlation between welcoming talented and freedom-loving immigrants and the prosperity of nations is not a coincidence: immigrants are a boon to our economies. It has been widely reported that the share of foreign-born residents has risen significantly in the United States. Such new residents comprised 10.4% of the total US population in 2000 (statistics available online at www.census.gov). Without these foreign-born neighbors in our great country, our economy would collapse. They serve as doctors, engineers, computer and software programmers, professors, construction workers, landscapers, nurses and nannies, hotel and restaurant workers. Without an open, albeit secure, border, we would lose the growth engine of our labor force and our economy.

Closing the border to new immigrants would be even more severe for Canada or Australia. Canada, our biggest trading partner, has a total fertility rate (average number of births per woman) nearly 25% below what is called the "replacement rate." In other words, each woman needs to average roughly 2.07 babies to *maintain* a population in the long-run, while Canada's average is 1.6. Interestingly, the United States' birth rate is just at the replacement rate, so we would not have growth in the long-run, but neither would we decline – our growth will come from new immigrants who migrate here to work hard, pay taxes, and live in freedom. Canada relies even more on new immigrants than the United States does in order to have some growth. Frankly, Canada is our ally and biggest trading partner – by far the greatest market for our exports, so I'm glad that their economy has grown very well over the last few years. I point out again that a lot of this growth is due to the brilliant immigrants who have been coming to Canada.

So let us keep our nation strong and vital by keeping our borders and our minds open to freedom-loving, talented, and hardworking immigrants.

Laws alone cannot secure freedom of expression;
in order that every man present his views without
penalty, there must be a spirit of tolerance
in the entire population.
Albert Einstein, 1950

RULE 9: *LOVE AND CHERISH ANY FREEDOM-LOVING, TOLERANT NEIGHBOR OF ANY RELIGION, RACE, NATIONAL ORIGIN, OR PEACEFUL PERSONAL PREFERENCES, AS THYSELF.*

This rule relates to the one before it. Just as we must keep our borders open and accept immigrants, we must embrace all our neighbors, regardless of their race, ethnicity, national origin, sexual orientation, and/or peaceful political and religious beliefs. Intolerance breeds further intolerance. Ultimately, intolerance is a root cause of the terrorist attacks. The terrorists' intolerance towards Americans and the world's admiration for our ideals and success led them to hijack our planes so that they might crash them into our symbols of freedom and prosperity. We can only speculate where the last plane, the United flight in which the passengers bravely took on the hijackers and attempted to regain control of the cockpit, was headed, but some say a second attack on Washington, DC was thwarted by these heroes. It pains me to hear religious leaders blaming our fellow Americans for the attack, suggesting that we are being punished in some way. Now is the time for religious leaders to help us cope with the tragedy, not turn us against each other. They should preach tolerance, as only tolerance leads to peace.

A true patriot will take this opportunity to support our Muslim-American fellow citizens. They mourn with us, having lost family members and loved ones on Sept. 11 no less than other Americans. Patronize their businesses, help them feel safe and secure by asking them to join you for shopping trips. This will not only further unite our nation, it also increases spending at a time when the economy needs it. Above all, let us not repeat the painful history of ostracizing our fellow citizens, as we did in the World War II years to our loyal Japanese citizens. I repeat, intolerance breeds violence, tolerance breeds unity and love and peace.

A common danger unites even the bitterest enemies.
Aristotle, 4th century BC

RULE 10: *WE CAN TAKE HEART THAT THE US ECONOMY WILL REBOUND SOON, DUE TO THESE POSITIVE FACTORS:*

Six key factors are falling now that will fuel a recovery in the US economy. Two factors we have discussed at length above: interest rates and the US$ foreign exchange rate. Interest rates are indeed falling even further, with Alan Greenspan announcing another cut in the Federal Funds Rate on October 2. This bold but needed action once again validated my rule above – we can count on an independent and patriotic Federal Reserve System. The series of Fed interest rate cuts will fuel consumer spending on a whole host of products and services. The value of the US$ fell as a direct result of the attack on America, as shown in Figure 5 below. For all the reasons we discussed above in Rule 2, a lower foreign exchange rate on the US$ can actually help us export more of our goods and thereby fuel a recovery in the manufacturing and agriculture sectors. So the terrorists' attempt to end US financial supremacy has instead unwittingly boosted US competitiveness.

We also discussed the impact of falling taxes above. Beyond the tax refund we received in 2001, it seems likely that additional targeted tax cuts will be on their way soon, putting more dollars in our pockets which we can then spend on goods and services produced in the US and in

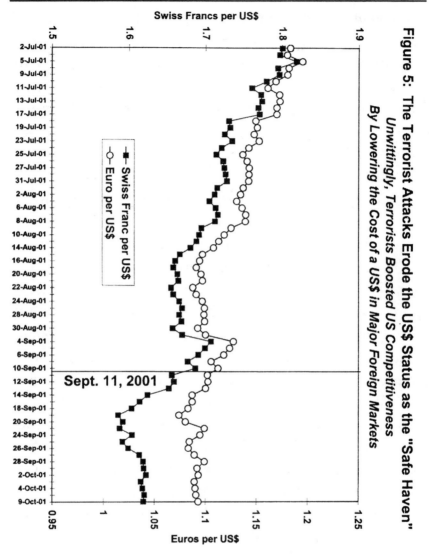

Figure 5: The Terrorist Attacks Erode the US$ Status as the "Safe Haven" Unwittingly, Terrorists Boosted US Competitiveness By Lowering the Cost of a US$ in Major Foreign Markets

our allied nations. Indeed, a temporary cut in payroll taxes will stimulate job creation for our furloughed or down-sized neighbors.

This relates to the fourth factor: falling bipartisan squabbling. As the nation unites, legislation to ease our recovery will pass through Congress easily. Leaders of both parties recognize that we are all Americans first and foremost, and now is the time to present a united face to the world. Republicans and Democrats in Congress will work together to authorize funds and other war-time measures to defeat terrorism and fuel US economic recovery.

The fifth factor, falling inventories, indicates that business will once again begin producing and investing in plants and equipment. A major point above is that we were in recession before the terrorist attack. Why? We had disappointingly low holiday sales from Thanksgiving onward last winter. Among other factors, a lot of people saw their 401K become a "201K" after the NASDAQ speculative bubble burst from its March 10, 2000 peak. Firms spent the bulk of 2001 cutting their production until the unsold inventories of goods were finally sold off their shelves. The slowdown in the US economy up to September 11 was largely attributable to the reductions in production that were needed to burn off excess inventory. Now that we have low inventories and the four factors above that argue for a pickup in spending, we should anticipate an increase in consumption but also in investment in new plant and equipment spending by firms, a key part of GDP as we discussed in Rule 2.

Sixth, energy prices have declined significantly, both from their peaks last winter, and from their already lowered prices, pre-September 11. One major theme of this book is that all nations and people of all religions, deserve the chance to join with us in the fight for a civilized freedom. OPEC nations, including many Islamic countries, have acted to spur the global economy by pumping plenty of oil. The resulting sharp decline in the oil price puts dollars in US consumers' pockets, as we now pay less at the pump and to heat our homes. Many firms also gain from reduced energy costs, so spending on non-energy items should rebound.

So we already have at least six positive signs that the US economy will rebound soon. I encourage each of you to continue to follow the economic trends in the news using some of the links I have given you here, and by accessing my own website, **globalguru.com**. I put updated graphs and commentary on this site, available completely free, as I see it as an extension of my teaching vocation.

The final message again for all of us is to get out there, not be afraid, travel, make purchases, refinance our homes, etc. In short, act now according to the rules of patriotic economics and you will secure freedom and prosperity for yourself, your loved ones, and your nation. Help America and its allies thrive by helping yourself – buy at low prices and interest rates!

Rule 11: *Patriotic executives "walk the talk:" if "our people are our most important asset," please work with them to avoid layoffs.*

Executives, particularly CEOs, are under tremendous pressure from investment analysts. Not all, but too many, analysts are myopic, asking CEOs questions such as "how are your current profits compared to earlier expectations?" without taking September 11 into account. Businesses and industries well beyond the obvious ones, e.g. travel-related, have been negatively impacted.

The key to our ability to restore economic growth and banish economic depression, however, may very well lie in how executives respond. If executives lay-off some of their employees, hoping to cut costs and boost short-term profits, they allow myopic analysts to push them into providing satisfaction to terrorists, by harming US families and the US economy.

Obviously, some industries were so directly impacted that they have no choice but to furlough some workers. I do not mean to criticize executives in those industries at such a stressful time. However, the salient point is that all executives should show faith in our future and make efforts to keep as many of their people on the payroll as is humanly possible. This could involve innovative solutions such as work-sharing (who wouldn't want a few more free hours each week?) or reduced wages for employees, as well as reduced salaries and no bonuses for executives.

Innovative solutions and a patriotic teamwork between "labor and management" are absolutely essential. We are at war against economic depression, as well as terrorism. The battle can be won if we minimize layoffs. For financial and psychological reasons, widespread layoffs do great damage. Notably, executives need to assure each other that they will not be "free riders." That is, they should not "cheat" the system by cutting their firm's headcount and thus costs while benefiting from a healthy / recovering economy as a result of other executives struggling to retain all their workers. This is a time for national resolve: executives must meet – perhaps through the US Chamber of Commerce or Business Roundtable – to assure each other that they will do their part to sustain employment and thus income and economic activity.

Jim Blanchard, the Chairman and CEO of Synovus Financial Corp., is one of America's foremost leaders. Synovus has over $15 billion in assets and maintains employment of roughly 10,000 people in a network of 38 Southeastern banks and at Total System Services, Inc. (TSYS). Synovus owns over 80% of TSYS, a leading electronic payment processor.

Importantly, both Synovus and TSYS have performed admirably for nearly two decades on the NYSE. This is crucial, as both firms have achieved highly-ranked financial returns through a justifiably acclaimed company culture which truly "walks the talk" (no layoffs as of late October) of valuing all their people. I can do no better than to share such a culture with you, directly from the heart and pen of the steward of the culture of TSYS and of Synovus.

Culture and Performance:
One Company's Perspective
by James H. Blanchard

Chairman and CEO

Synovus Financial Corp.

Bill Turner, a member of our company's founding family, likes to tell this story about an interview he once had with a "big city" reporter. After many questions and answers, the reporter still didn't comprehend the "Culture of the Heart" that sets Synovus apart.

"Listen," Mr. Turner finally said, "you obviously don't want to hear this. Or maybe you think it's a disguise for something else. But our company's culture is really all about love - open, sincere, unconditional love."

It has taken employers more than a few decades to realize that work – profitable, fulfilling, life-changing work – starts with *people* who are fulfilled. There's a tangible connection between a company's culture and its performance. Executives are only now beginning to realize that the best ideas about work and leadership aren't the newest. In fact, they're the very oldest ideas.

In 2001, the Synovus family of companies was named #8 on FORTUNE magazine's list of the "100 Best Companies to Work for in America." This is the third consecutive year we have been in the national "Top 10". We were named #1 in 1999. I have said over and over again that I am not sure we are the best or even the eighth best place to work in America, but it certainly is a grand affirmation of our culture and our commitment to be a great place to work. I know we *want* to be the best place to work. I know we are committed to being a great place to work. I know we want, as much as anything else, to be a place where people feel loved. We want to be a place where people trust their leaders, where they feel like they are in a safe place, a fun place, a rewarding place, a challenging place and a place where they know that there is somebody – even several people – that really gives a darn about them. That's the *Culture of the Heart.*

In any company, people are the most important asset. People may choose companies based on a checklist of perks and benefits, but they choose to stay because of that company's culture. Many companies can buy the benefits found at the best companies to work for in America. The difference at Synovus is our *Culture of the Heart* that bonds everything and everyone together. Without a pervasive culture of concern and respect, those benefits amount to little more than a list on paper.

In the midst of an information revolution, the real battle on the front lines of business is not for technology. Companies across all sectors are waging the hardest fights for talented people.

That's certainly the case at Total System Services, Inc., one of the world's leading payment transaction processors in which Synovus owns a predominant (80.8%) interest. In fewer than 20 years, TSYS has grown from a small department to a publicly-traded company of more than 5,000 team members who service more than 200 million cardholder accounts for over 300 million consumers.

Because our people love their jobs, the Company continues to grow and we are still flooded with hundreds of applicants every week. We don't just hire people, we find team members who want to join a family and stay with us. Annual turnover among most companies is 26 percent, but it's dropped to 12 percent on average at Synovus companies. I believe that's a phenomenal illustration of our culture at work in the most competitive talent sectors of business today.

We teach leaders how to nurture and protect thriving on-the-job relationships with the team members they serve. We teach every team leader in the Company how to live the values, share the vision, make others successful and manage the business. We teach leaders how to match each person's career goals with our corporate goals, so team members are engaged in the Company's success and control their own development.

We offer great benefits that make a real difference in people's lives because it's the right thing to do. Our team members believe that their company believes in them, even in tough times. Happy, productive, motivated people produce outstanding results. They just do!

So it should be clear that culture works. We've often said that if we could apply only one rule in our company it would be the Golden Rule. If every one of us would treat every other person we come in contact with like we would want to be treated, Synovus would be the #1 company in the world in every category that could be evaluated.

You may be thinking why should a company do all these things for its people? After all, we pay them and they owe us something in return. This is a logical question and one I will try to address. First, it is the right thing to do. Go back to what I just said about the Golden Rule. People deserve and respond positively to being cared for and loved. In fact, it brings out the best in most people, which is the second reason. It has been proven over and over that people will try harder and give more of themselves when they feel cared for, respected and appreciated. When the best is brought out in employees, they care more about the company, which shows up in how they treat customers and their work effort. We all know when our customers receive the highest level of service and enjoy interacting with a company's employees, the end result tends to be increased repeat business and sales, which ultimately results in increased returns for shareholders.

Additionally, in difficult times like these, I believe our employees can be a tremendously positive force in our communities. Through their caring for customers and positive outlook, they can provide reassurance and hope.

In essence, the foundation we help provide for our employees is shared with everyone we come in contact with every day! I believe any company can be great when a few people choose to make it great, and take 100 percent responsibility for making a difference in the lives of the people they work with. There's no deep mystery here: *A culture is built one decision at a time, one day at a time, one relationship at a time.*

Summing Up:

How to Thrive While Helping America

This book has a dual purpose. I want to help citizens throughout the world who have faith in the future and the desire to improve their financial position despite these troubled and uncertain times. I also want to help my own country and the nations who step up as allies for freedom and tolerance, by proposing a positive, yet realistic, set of rules for a renewed prosperity.

The beauty of these new rules is that there are not the usual trade-offs that lead many to call economics the "dismal science." Here, I propose new rules that show how you can thrive as individuals through actions which also help the allied nations. Indeed, after the tactical war is won by the brave forces of the allied nations, strategic war will only be won if we have a vision to fight what will be the ultimate war of the 21st century: the war on global poverty and hunger. This is why calls for a "new Marshall Plan" are a great strategy, and actions such as simultaneous dropping of food along with military operations from October 7 onwards show that the allied nations care about the freedom and welfare of all the world's people.

I have shown throughout this book how you can thrive individually by following these new rules. The main point is that anyone with financial means or security should be buying, both products and stocks or mutual funds. Those without a lot of cash but with good future prospects can be borrowing at historically-low interest rates. The final graph summarizes how YOU can thrive by having the courage and patriotism to follow the new rules.

Figure 6 shows that a steady strategy of investing a fixed-dollar amount into mutual funds every month should prove to be the best long-run investment. Two key trends

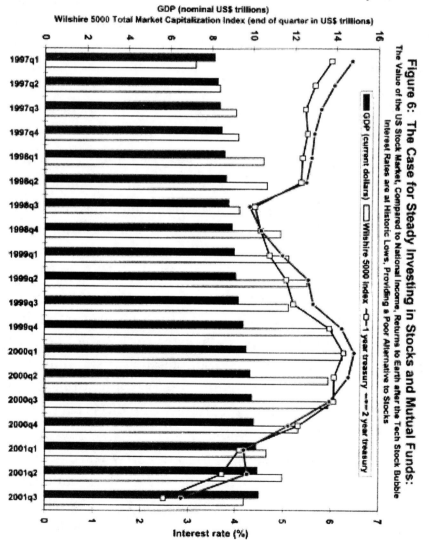

Figure 6: The Case for Steady Investing in Stocks and Mutual Funds: The Value of the US Stock Market, Compared to National Income, Returns to Earth after the Tech Stock Bubble Interest Rates are at Historic Lows, Providing a Poor Alternative to Stocks

are emerging that substantiate this strong claim. First, notice that interest rates on alternative investments, such as treasury notes that are fairly safe because they will mature in one or two years, have been driven down to historically low levels. Fearful people buy them as "safe havens" but the result is returns (i.e. interest rates) so low that after tax they will not even keep up with inflation.

The second key trend evident in Figure 6 is that the market has corrected for the speculative bubble that made stocks, in hindsight, obviously overvalued or expensive up to the peaks during 2000. At least through the summer of 2001, our economy grew, and inflation continued to increase the nominal value of US GDP. Thus, the total stock market value of US headquartered firms, as proxied by the Wilshire 5000 Index, is once again below the value of our annual national income (GDP). This is not a full model of valuation. However, when you put these two trends together, the low interest rates on any alternative investment and the attractive value of the US stock market compared to our national income, I think you will agree that Figure 6 validates my main point: buy American, buy from our allies, buy stocks and mutual funds and hold them for the long-run. Why? You can do well financially while doing good patriotically.

GOD BLESS AMERICA IN ALL ITS DYNAMIC DIVERSITY; E PLURIBUS UNUM.